from Jesus

Brief messages of encouragement from Jesus,
to help people realise what God offers them

Marie E. Page

OPENBOOK
PUBLISHERS

To my family,
and all God's family.

'He is our strength and our song.'

The Scripture texts are taken from *The Holy Bible*:
New International Version, © 1973, 1978, 1984 by the
International Bible Society.

Cover photograph: Ian Morris

First printing January 1991
02 01 00 99 98 97 96   12 11 10 9 8 7 6

National Library of Australia
Cataloguing-in-Publication entry

Page, Marie E.
    Personal messages from Jesus.

    ISBN 0 85910 572 5.

    1. Bible – Meditations. I. Title

242'.5

Copyright © 1991
Openbook Publishers
205 Halifax Street, Adelaide, South Australia   1507-95

Psalm 46   Isaiah 55:8,9   Hebrews 10:22

Be still, and know that I am God. Psalm 46:10

Yield to me, your Lord; yield to my power that is always ready to work for you.

Do not strive in your own strength. Come to me, submit to me, trust in me. Look to me always — I am within you, ready to bear your every burden. Remember Calvary; when you bear your own burdens you do not glorify the work I did on Calvary, where I shed my blood for you.

It saddens me when I see my children struggling on their own, when they leave my side, when they are unable to trust completely. Always remember: I am your shield, your refuge, your help, and I am there even when troubles come to you, for your own good, for your growth — which is for my glory.

Cease to strive in your own strength. Allow me to do the work. Be still, rest, trust, and allow me to work my plans out in your life, in your household.

My ways are not your way; my ways are perfect and performed with a loving hand. Remember: there is no greater love than mine.

Ephesians 4:2–6   Mark 11:25,26
Matthew 22:37–40   Luke 6:37,38

There is one body and one Spirit — just as you were called to one hope when you were called. Ephesians 4:4

I call you to unity. Since you were baptised into me, you and all believers are one body — my body on earth. And when you receive my Supper, you participate in my body and blood.

I call you to forgive, for in forgiving you also are forgiven.

I call you to love your neighbour as yourself, for in loving your neighbour you love me, as I first loved you.

I call you to give, for in giving you give to me, as I have given to you.

I call you to die to self, to submit to my hand, for in dying to self you die for me, as I first died for you.

The triumph of Calvary continues on in my body when you obey my Word.

Give all, and you shall receive all.

Whoever follows me will never walk in darkness, but will have the light of life. John 8:12

I am the light of the world, and my kingdom will have no end.

Do not stop praising me. Praise is the weapon against a great cloud of darkness descending upon the world.

Be my light amid this darkness; allow my hand to be upon you, and my light to be within you.

Remain passive in my moulding hands, trusting. Then, and only then, does my light shine from within you. Shine amid the darkness of the world.

As a lighthouse shows its light to the lost ships in the night, so my light shines to the lost of the world.

As never before, I call you to trust. I call you to a way of complete submission and obedience. Trust me, and remain passive amid the many storms you will face. Remember: I am the King, master of all things, and my ways are perfect. I will never leave you, nor will I ever forsake you.

Remember, too, there is no greater love than my love for you. I want more for you than you want for yourself. I know your every need.

Matthew 6:33   Isaiah 45:5–8   Psalm 91:1–6

Let the earth open wide, let salvation spring up, let righteousness grow with it; I, the Lord, have created it. Isaiah 45:8

Seek first my kingdom and my righteousness, and all things shall be yours as well. All glory and honour are mine; I am the King, and the keeper and giver of all things.

The heavens, the earth, the seas, and all the wonders in them were made through me. I am your Creator — I made you in love, and in love I died for you. I died that you may receive grace upon grace, blessing upon blessing — that you may be free in me.

Have faith in this love, believe in my righteousness. Draw near to me daily, giving thanks for all things, and trusting.

Open your eyes to my creation — wonder at the wonders I have done. Be as little children, and see me and seek me amid the glories I have placed on the earth and within the heavens for you.

Have faith in my faithfulness, in my righteousness. I am your refuge and hiding place. With your eyes upon me, be as trusting as little children, and I will surely guide you and keep you safely beneath my wings.

2 Corinthians 6:4–10   Hebrews 12:5–12
Matthew 7:13,14

If we died with him, we will also live with him;
if we endure, we will also reign with him.
2 Timothy 2:11,12

Endure; I call you to endure for my name's sake.

When I permit sufferings of body, mind, and spirit to touch my children, remember that I have suffered for you, and that I am with you in your suffering.

Submit to my dealings, to my hand of discipline, for it is a loving hand. Yield to my will for you.

My desire is to strengthen you, to deepen your faith in me, your Saviour, so that you run the race of faith and receive eternal life.

Remember: The gate to eternal life is narrow.

With prayer, praise, and thanksgiving, offer back to me the burdens I permit you to bear. Accept my peace, that your joy may be made full, and trust me as I lead you through the narrow gate.

Do you not know that your body is a temple of the Holy Spirit, who is in you, whom you have received from God? You are not your own; you were bought at a price. Therefore, honour God with your body. 1 Corinthians 6:19,20

You are the temple of God, my holy vessel. I seek to work in you and through you, but first you must be cleansed and made free to serve my purposes.

Tenderly, I cleanse you and set you free. Tenderly, I remove past pains, the hurts in your life.

Tenderly, I remove layer upon layer.

Tenderly, I begin to buff and shine you.

Tenderly, as new grime gathers, I buff and shine again.

I dwell deep within your being. I seek to remove all things from you that would dull my light from being reflected in you.

Tenderly, and in love, I renew my children. My child, be loving to me by being tender and loving to other people.

Acts 20:35   Philippians 4:8,9
1 Thessalonians 5:11–15

*Live in harmony with one another; be
sympathetic, love as brothers, be
compassionate and humble. Do not repay
evil with evil or insult with insult, but with
blessing, because to this you were called so
that you may inherit a blessing. 1 Peter 3:8,9*

Do not seek gain for yourself, but rather allow me
to cultivate within you an attitude of giving of
yourself to others.

Offer thoughts and words that will always bring peace:
kind thoughts toward others; words flowing with
love, giving encouragement, always building up.
Even a stern word that is spoken in love can
build up, bring peace, and give hope.

Always be a peacemaker, for I come to bring peace.

These things can come only from a humble heart.
Humility shows the fruits of the Spirit.

If you desire these, then yield to me, obey me. Then I
will cleanse your heart and make you my
peacemaker, bringing blessings to others, as you
yourself have been blessed.

Psalm 27:4,5   Lamentations 3:22–24
Psalm 36:5,6   Hebrews 13:8

It is good to wait quietly for the salvation of the Lord. Lamentations 3:26

Come and sit with me, and look upon my beauty; be still before me. Allow me to bathe you in my loving-kindness. Like spring flowers and softly falling rain, my loving hands will touch you.

Always rest in the knowledge that I am love. I am with you as you stroll peacefully through a green meadow of flowers, and I never leave your side as you go onward through the rocks and thistles.

Always be assured of my faithfulness, mercy, and forgiveness, for when you seem to fall, I am with you. When the flowers no longer bloom, and the green meadow turns to dust, I am with you.

When the breeze is no longer gentle, and you are tossed and turned by the winds, I am with you.

Though the seasons change, I never change. I am your Saviour, now and forever.

2 Corinthians 1:3,4 Psalm 125:1
Ephesians 1:22,23

*You are the ruler of all things. In your hands
are strength and power to exalt and give
strength to all. 1 Chronicles 29:12*

I am the Father of all mercy, the God of all comfort.
My nature is love, and I have an infinite love for
my children.

Believe in this love; have faith and a trust in me that is
unwavering, like a mountain that cannot be
moved.

Your life is in my loving hands.

In love I send the sunshine.

In love I send the storms.

Welcome also the storms — the sunshine and new
growth will follow, and my desire is for you to
grow in me.

Remember: all things are under my feet — so trust me
always, my child.

1 Chronicles 16:28–34 Zechariah 7:8–10
Psalm 47:1–7 Matthew 5:34–40

Worship the Lord in the splendour of his holiness. 1 Chronicles 16:29

Come, worship me in the beauty of my holiness. Worship me in music and song, with clapping hands, in prayer, in silent adoration and thanksgiving; but remember that true worship comes only from a worshipful heart.

Worship me in trust and obedience.

Worship me with a heart that is gentle.

Worship me with tenderness and caring for your brothers and sisters, comforting the broken-hearted; worship me by loving the unlovable.

Be my mouth, my hands, my feet; be my light to others in their darkness.

When you tend them, you tend me.

When you love them, you love me.

When you give to them, you give to me.

Come! worship me.

Psalm 37:3–6   Jeremiah 17:7,8   Isaiah 43:1,2

Trust in the Lord with all your heart and lean not on your own understanding; in all your ways acknowledge him, and he will make your paths straight. Proverbs 3:5,6

Trust me! All things are in my hands. I am your King, your source. Trust in my love, for I am yours and you are mine.

When you trust in me, troubles and difficulties will not harm you. In me you will find refreshment.

Do not look around and say: 'I don't understand'. Do not lean on your own understanding, on what you see — only trust in me. I will show you the way to go.

You are covered in my love. Bathe in this love, for I cherish you. I know you by name, and you are my child. I will see you through deep waters, when the light is dim.

Take my hand, trust in me, walk with me.

Proverbs 23:15,16   Matthew 15:18–20
Colossians 3:17

*Create in me a pure heart, O God, and renew
a steadfast spirit within me. Psalm 51:10*

From the mouth come the thoughts of your heart.

From the heart come forth attitudes and actions.

Daily open your heart to me completely, and allow me
to cleanse it and make it new.

Then your heart, as a mirror, will reflect godliness in
your speech.

Your heart will reflect a right attitude, leading to right
actions.

My desire for my children is that every thought, every
word, every deed, be in obedience to me,
bearing fruit for my kingdom. Do it all through the
power I give you, trusting in me.

Deuteronomy 10:12,13 1 John 2:3–6
Proverbs 2:1–6

The word of God is living and active. Sharper than any double-edged sword, it penetrates even to dividing soul and spirit, joints and marrow; it judges the thoughts and attitudes of the heart. Hebrews 4:12

Obey me, obey my word. Saturate yourself in my word. My word is indeed sharper than a two-edged sword, that pierces to the deepest marrow — if you so allow it.

To know me is to know my word — I am the living Word.

To know my word is to know of my deep love and forgiveness, to know of my power and judgments.

I call people to a way of unquestioning obedience.

I call people to know and understand the fear of the Lord, to realise my awesome wonder. To know it leads to life, wisdom, and understanding.

Trust in my faithfulness and mercy. Know that when you fall on the road of obedience, I am there to pick you up and place you on the straight path.

Come, walk the way of trust and obedience, the way of the living Word, for I have saved you.

Isaiah 55:1   John 4:11–15   Colossians 1:15–17

Let him who hears say, 'Come'. Whoever is thirsty, let him come; and whoever wishes, let him take the free gift of the water of life. Revelation 22:17

Come to me. I am the living water, the fountain of life. Come and live in me, play in me. Let me be your joy and trust — your resting place. In me find cleansing and refreshment.

I am a spring of flowing water, bringing eternal life.

Drink deeply of my living water; drink of me. Exist through me, as all things came into existence through me and for me.

Allow the living water to heal you, to soothe you, to bring you tranquillity, to bring new life.

Come, my child, drink of me.

Psalm 91:14   Jeremiah 7:23   Acts 5:29

The eternal God is your refuge, and
underneath are the everlasting arms.
Deuteronomy 33:27

D o not keep striving and struggling. Let me carry
you over the highways and byways. Come and
shelter in the shadow of my wings, as together
we walk.

Trust in me. I will protect you and shelter you from
storms and dangers.

Allow me to raise you to higher places. You may ask:
'What are higher places, Lord?'

To walk higher, my child, is to walk in the simplicity of
my love, to be obedient and forever trusting, with
a childlike faith.

For even when human beings oppose you, I will lead
you and give you strength.

Isaiah 55:10–12   Ephesians 4:1,2   Galatians 6:2

Rejoice in the Lord always. I will say it again:
Rejoice! Let your gentleness be evident to all.
Philippians 4:4

Be my bell-ringers — ring joy-bells for me to others. Be my happiness-makers, as I have brought happiness to you.

My mission is to bring happiness. Let the angel's announcement of good tidings flow from your words and actions.

I have come to bring peace, and forgiveness, and comfort to all people.

Be joyful children, telling others of the joyful things of my word. Tell them what I have done for them, and how much I love them. Show kindness, comfort those in sorrow, bear others' burdens, cheer those who are sad and weary, and scatter fragments of my love, joy, and peace wherever you go.

1 John 5:3–5   1 Peter 4:12,13   1 John 4:4

Everyone born of God has overcome the world. This is the victory that has overcome the world, even our faith. 1 John 5:4

B e overcomers! I have overcome the world, and through faith in me you have my power. The daily trials and conflicts I send are testings of your growth and strength in me.

As you would exercise your muscles to gain greater physical strength, so too you must exercise faith in me, so that your trust may grow.

Be as a green stick in my hand — be flexible.

Allow me to bend you; you know that I will never break you. Should there be a little pain, rejoice, because you are sharing in my sufferings and growing in me.

The greatest form of worship you can show me is a deepening faith and trust. I am in you, and I am greater than all who oppose you.

Proverbs 29:26   Galatians 6:1   Job 33:4

Stop judging by mere appearances, and make a right judgment. John 7:24

I say: 'Do not judge others'. But where you have to judge, then judge by the yardstick of goodness and love. Only I can judge truly, and I show goodness and love.

I say to you: Be patient with others, show compassion. Love the sinner, but hate the sin. Ask for my love, and I will give it to you. Remember that you too may be tempted, and without me you would fall.

Look and see me in everyone. I made all people and all things. Therefore I am in that person who seems to you to be the most lowly.

Each and every one of you is my unique creation — each is a part of me. And I have died on the cross for each one of you.

So never judge someone I created and died for, from evil motives, but always judge in love, for I am love.

**1 Corinthians 11:1 Matthew 6:14,15 1 John 3:14
Matthew 7:3**

*If you forgive men when they sin against you,
your heavenly Father will also forgive you.
Matthew 6:14*

Follow my example. Always forgive those who wrong
you in any way, as your Father in heaven has
forgiven you. Don't allow hate, envy, pride, and
jealousy to build up in your heart. Talk to me
about those logs in your eye; confess them — I
see them anyway, and I know how they hurt you.
Ask me, and I will clear your eye.

I know and understand what it is to be beaten and to
be accused. I understand your human nature.
Ask for my grace to forgive and love others.

Always do your best in whatever circumstance you
find yourself — always be willing to do my will.
Desire to die to self and self-centredness, and
then look to me, the faithful one, to do the work
within you.

Joshua 1:6–18   Proverbs 14:27
1 Corinthians 10:13   Hebrews 13:6–8

Do not fear, for I am with you; do not be dismayed, for I am your God. I will strengthen you and help you. Isaiah 41:10

B e strong and courageous; determine to do my will. I have made you mine, and I give you my strength. So when I ask, choose to obey.

So often, every fibre of your human nature and your human reasoning will rebel, and fear. Place your will in mine, choose to die to self, my child — allow me to be your strength.

Do not fear your human fear, your emotions; only have the fear of the Lord, a trusting commitment to me. I know you, I made you, I understand and love you. I am love, I am understanding, I am all things; and I will never ask you to take one more step without first preparing you and giving you the strength you need.

You may ask: 'What is your will for me, Lord?' My will is always in accordance with my word. I am the same yesterday, today, and forever.

Psalm 51:5–10   Psalm 94:12   Luke 6:45

God demonstrates his own love for us in this:
While we were still sinners, Christ died for us.
Romans 5:8

I am Love. I came in love, I died in love for you, even when you had rejected me. I discipline and train you in love. All my plans, ways, and actions are love; my fathomless depths are love.

Always consider your words and actions. Carefully consider the motives of your heart. Are they really in my name? A right action may be performed with a wrong motive. A right word may be spoken with no love in the heart — with a wrong motive.

But there can also be wrong words and actions with a right motive, based on love in the heart. Solid growth is slow — do not despair! Put your trust in me, and daily desire to increase in me.

In the final day, all things that don't measure up to love will be blown away. Depend on my love; love your neighbour, and love me.

Luke 18:16,17   1 Corinthians 15:58   Psalm 31:19

Let the little children come to me, and do not hinder them, for the kingdom of God belongs to such as these. Luke 18:16

I ask you to be like little children before me. I am asking you to have the simplicity of a small child, and a childlike trust — a trust that is steadfast and uncomplicated.

To those who are childlike I give the kingdom of God.

I ask that there be tenderness, purity, and candour. Have a stillness within your spirit that gives birth to absolute surrender and submission to me. Totally rest in my love and goodness for you, by just sitting and talking with me in childlike trust — by being my close friend, and allowing me to be yours.

I want to give so much to you. Do not resist, but let me bless you, as your loving Father.

These are some of the things I'm saying when I exhort you: 'Be like little children'.

1 John 5:13,20   Isaiah 40:31   Revelation 21:4

I write these things to you who believe in the name of the Son of God so that you may know that you have eternal life. 1 John 4:13

Measure everything against eternity, since in me you have eternal life.

I know that even a day may seem so long to you; it may seem almost endless. You strive as though time was ending, as though all — every reward and every blessing — must be gained now.

My child, time for you has no ending. Ponder on this. Measure an earthly lifetime against eternity, and it is but a breath.

As on the wings of an eagle, rise above earthly worries; soar on trust and submission. Look down as if from above, and realise that your whole life on earth is no more than one grain of sand in the whole ocean.

I am with you forever as your God, and I will wipe away every tear from your eyes. All the old problems will disappear.

2 Corinthians 3:4–6   John 12:24–28
Romans 6:3–8

In all these things we are more than
conquerors through him who loved us.
Romans 8:37

In yourself you are nothing, but in me you have
completeness, all things. Grow daily in trust of
me, your Saviour.

Don't be afraid to submit totally to me. Look again at
Calvary, ponder on my sufferings and my blood I
shed for you. While you were still a sinner, I
totally submitted to the will of the Father, and I
died for you. And through your baptism you
shared in my death, and you also share in the
freedom of my resurrection.

Submit and take hold of the blessings which I give
you. Let there be complete abandonment to me
in all you are and all you have.

Nothing is yours; and yet all is yours, through me.
Give yourself to me, be crucified in me, and rise
with me. It is a daily process. Be a conqueror
through me. Through me you possess all.

John 15:4–11   John 14:21–27   Philippians 4:11–13
1 John 2:15–17

Peace I leave with you; my peace I give you
... Do not let your hearts be troubled and do
not be afraid. John 14:27

R emain in me. Stay close to me in your thoughts.
Let me fill your heart.

Take my peace. It is not a worldly peace I give you; it's
a peace that is deep within you — that shows
itself in your love and obedience of me.

My peace comes when you are humble and depend
on me, knowing you can do nothing without me,
knowing you are nothing without me. It means
feeling contentment in the midst of discomfort
and turmoil, knowing that your strength comes
from me.

I long to give this peace to you, to serve all. But those
who cling to worldly standards and goals, those
who depend on themselves and do not put their
trust in me in their lives, cannot receive.

Only those who know me, and continually remain in
me and my love, share in my peace.

John 11:25,26   Romans 6:4–8
1 Thessalonians 5:23,24   Hebrews 9:13,14

I have been crucified with Christ and I no longer live, but Christ lives in me. The life I live in the body, I live by faith in the Son of God, who loved me and gave himself for me.
Galatians 2:20

I am your resurrection and life. I give you newness of life through faith in me. In me you have death of your old self and new life. You see, you live to die, and you die to live.

Your renewing, and your dying to self, my child, is a continuing work. You were baptised into my death, and each day through faith you die and rise again with me. I now live in you.

I want to sanctify you, to enrich you, but you must allow me to work in you. You see, I am gentle; I never force myself upon you. Rather, I beckon you to come to me — to follow me.

Through my sacrificial death you are sanctified to follow me, and in following me you are sanctified — I ask you to come!

Philippians 4:4–7   Psalm 55:22,23   Colossians 4:2
Romans 8:31

*Do not be anxious about anything, but in
everything, by prayer and petition, with
thanksgiving, present your requests to God.*
Philippians 4:6

Rejoice in me, and do not be anxious about
anything. O my child, if only you could grasp this
truth and hold on to it! The truth is that I'm
waiting for you to come to me with all your
perplexities and troubles, to take care of them.
How large or how small they may be is not
important.

Come before me in prayer; speak to me openly and
confidently. A few simple words that come from
the heart are heard in heaven.

Know that I am for you, and if I am for you, who or
what could be against you? Do not doubt my
faithfulness; doubt builds walls between hearts
— between your heart and mine.

When you trust in me, my power flows to you. It drives
out doubt and anxiety, and then your heart is
filled with my peace, which is beyond
understanding.

**Mark 14:32–36   James 1:2–4   Romans 8:15–17
Isaiah 30:15**

You received the Spirit of sonship. And by him we cry, 'Abba, Father'. Romans 8:15

Pray to God as your loving Father — learn to say 'Abba, Father' from your heart.

In the garden of Gethsemane, as I waited for my time to come, my soul grieved to the point of death. Only by submitting to my Father's will, saying 'Abba, Father, your will, not mine', did I have peace and the strength to face my suffering and death.

My grace does not take trial out of daily living; you may still face criticisms, physical hardships, and sorrows. My child, use these as a stairway; with my help, climb to greater growth and trust.

Do not fight the storm; rather, ride on the winds, and flow with the high tides; and when in the eye of the storm, utter, with love in your heart: 'Abba, Father, may your will be done in me'.

You may still feel the blast, but a peace will come and keep your spirit calm and tranquil. You will be given an inner strength, so that you may endure it.

John 3:16 Isaiah 53:1–9 Matthew 26:26–28
Psalm 57:1–3

This is my blood of the covenant, which is poured out for many for the forgiveness of sins. Matthew 26:28

I have given myself for you; love me and delight in me, delight to do my will.

Rejoice in me; don't look upon me as only judge and King. I want you to come to me, to receive me, to have a personal relationship with me. Know me as your loving friend and Saviour, one who loves you and wishes to bless and accomplish all for you.

I love you so much that I came as the Father's only Son into the world to dwell among you. I came as a Son who lived a hard humble existence on earth, a Son who was forsaken, mocked, scourged, crowned with thorns, and then finally hung on a cross and died for you. I died that you might be forgiven of your sins and gain salvation.

I gave my body and shed my blood on the cross, and I offer you my body and blood in my Supper.

I ask only for your trust in me — a trust that makes your obedience and submission become a joy for you, and as incense to me.

Luke 16:10–12 2 Corinthians 5:20,21
Romans 4:18–21

*Whoever can be trusted with very little can
also be trusted with much. Luke 16:10*

B e obedient to me in small things, faithful in deeds
which may seem unimportant to you. There will
be crowns of glory for the martyrs who, through
the ages, have died rather than deny me as Lord.
But there will also be rewards for those who are
patient and unquestioning in what may appear, to
the world, a lowly service.

My child, be faithful in what I ask you to do and where
I place you. Be diligent, always do your best.
Remember, you are my ambassador.

Whether it is in some spiritual service, or applying your
skills in an office, toiling in the earth, in the home,
or in dull and routine work, I see it all. Do it all
faithfully, in my name.

Always be considerate to others; a smile may uplift a
fallen heart, and a kind word may bring comfort
to some lost soul.

The world may not see your deeds; you may be
unpraised in the eyes of other people; but I see
faithful obedient hearts. It is a faithful and
obedient heart which brings glory to me — not
the size of the action.

John 15:12–15   Colossians 3:12–17   Galatians 6:1

Greater love has no-one than this, that he lay down his life for his friends. John 15:13

Love one another as I have loved you. I am not speaking of sentimental love, but of a love which is committed to serve.

I call on you to love the unlovable, and to lay down your life for your friends — not in the physical sense, but to be dependable, loyal, and compassionate; to be patient with the impatient, kind to the unkind, gentle to the harsh, forgiving to the unforgiving, faithful to the unfaithful; to bear each others' burdens, always caring, and considering the other as greater than yourself.

Build each other up, rather than tearing them down.

Speak words of edification and encouragement.

Be understanding; if one among you takes a wrong path, endeavour to gently lead that person back.

Be discerning, but not judgmental; for who has not trod a wrong path? And who may be the next?

Ephesians 4:15,16 1 Corinthians 12:14–26
Isaiah 53:10

You are the body of Christ, and each one of you is a part of it. 1 Corinthians 12:27

Y ou are one body with all believers; be one in me, moving together, and not considering one part more important than another. If one part doesn't move with the others, then there is a breakdown, and the whole body suffers.

Love one another, as I first loved you. It is this love, this godly love, that holds the body together. My love must flow freely, as my blood flowed freely for each of you. And be continually strengthened by my body and my blood, given and shed for you.

It was because of my love for you that I died, that I was nailed to that cross for your sins. I was pleased to be crushed; I gladly became a sacrifice for your sins.

My child, love other people as I loved you. Set each other free, set my body free — be my disciples.

Luke 6:46–49   James 1:22–27   Proverbs 3:27–30
James 2:14–26

*Do not merely listen to the word, and so
deceive yourselves. Do what it says. James
1:22*

Hear my word; allow me to write it within your
heart. Allow me to soften your heart, so that, like
a sponge, it absorbs my word.

Act on my word; be a doer. Don't be an empty vessel,
but be an available instrument, a channel for me
to work through, to reach the broken ones, those
who cry alone in their darkness, those who live in
the barren desert — the ones people turn away
from. I desire to bring them to green pasture; but
you must carry my staff and show them the way.

Through you, let them see my compassion, my infinite
tenderness and forgiveness, my unchanging
goodness and mercy.

Pray for them, and answer your own requests for them
in all practical ways, such as a kind word, an ear
ready to listen, perhaps a letter, food, or warm
clothing.

Always be gentle. Do not be afraid to get your hands
dirty — my hands were calloused and worn before
they were pierced. I worked weary long hours for
you and for all people. My child, take my staff,
walk the way of the cross, be a doer of my word
— live out my gospel.

Matthew 11:28–30   Psalm 34:4–7
Romans 8:35–39

My God will meet all your needs according to his glorious riches in Christ Jesus. Philippians 4:19

C ome to me, all you who are heavy laden, and I will give you rest.

O my children, if you only knew how I wait for you to come to me, if you only understood my gentleness, my simplicity and humility, you would never be afraid to approach me, and to trust me in all your ways.

I see so many hearts weighed down under heavy loads, bearing their own burdens, floundering in their own way. I long for you to come to me, to take the load from you, and to give rest to your souls.

My love is far more than a human love; it is infinite, total, and perfect, and yet this is the simplicity of it. Trust me to take care of your every need. Even in the midst of trial I am with you; my angels and my love surround you.

Nothing — not even tribulation, famine, persecution, distress of any kind — absolutely nothing, not even death itself, can ever separate you from my love. Believe this; trust me in all things, in all your ways, and permit me to give rest to your souls.

Psalm 119:1–34,105   Psalm 63:1–3
Romans 11:33–36

The unfolding of your words gives light; it gives understanding to the simple. Psalm 119:130

Seek me with all your heart; delight in me, delight in my word; learn of my love.

My child, I give my word for your instruction, to guide you in the ways of righteousness, to light the path you tread, to be as a lamp at your feet, to keep you from stumbling into darkness. Seek me in my word, opening your heart to my Spirit. I will teach you and give you understanding.

My word is not just for the wise, the great teachers and scholars. It is written that even the simple be given wisdom and understanding. Open your heart to me and my word — I promise to fill it, I wait to fill it.

Love me in my word. I speak to each of my children personally; listen and learn of my loving-kindness, my unsearchable ways, my incomparable gentleness, and my glory. Each one of you is my special child — my love is big enough for that.

Walk in my ways, stay close to me, be one with me.

Isaiah 53:7–9 Galatians 2:20 1 Timothy 6:12
2 Timothy 4:7,8

*Consider him who endured such opposition
from sinful men, so that you will not grow
weary and lose heart. Hebrews 12:3*

Trust in me always; have faith in the Son of God
who died for you. Because of my love for you,
without a word of protest I gladly placed myself
into the hands of those who wanted to kill me.
They led me away, and in obedience to the
Father I permitted myself to be subjected to
torture and great humiliation, before they finally
slaughtered me.

It was for this death I came; it was my greatest
triumph, for in this way victory over sin was won.

My child, ponder on my earthly life and death. There
were times when I had nowhere to lay my head.
Consider my struggle, the battle over sin; rejoice
and give thanks for the victory.

With faith in me, take hold of your daily temptations
and conflicts, and turn them into victory. Not to
struggle is not to grow. Remember: the art of
warfare is learnt amid conflict. Without struggle
and conflict, there are no crowns; my reward is
for those who endure to the end.

Matthew 6:25–33   Matthew 10:30,31
Psalm 50:10,11   Psalm 139:1–6

[Your Father] causes his sun to rise on the evil and the good, and sends rain on the righteous and the unrighteous. Matthew 5:45

Trust me to provide for you. I know your every need; I know, too, the climate in which your growth into my likeness will most flourish. I know when sunshine, storm, soft intermittent rain, and dry times are needed.

I give food to the birds of the air, I clothe the flowers in all their splendour, I provide for the cattle on a thousand hills. They are all mine, and you are mine.

I supply sunshine and rain to all people, including those who choose to walk the path of rebellion. Don't doubt my love, my word, that I will give abundant blessings to you, my child. I know the number of hairs on your head. I know when you sit and when you rise, I know your every thought, your every desire; I am intimately acquainted with all your ways.

Believe in my love and compassion. Always trust me; walk in faith, and yield to what I know is best for you. I love you; let faith in me be your response.

Proverbs 15:1,2   Proverbs 17:27,28
Proverbs 18:20,21   James 3:3–12

Let your conversation be always full of grace,
seasoned with salt, so that you may know
how to answer everyone. Colossians 4:6

There is life and death in the power of the tongue.

Always be gentle and loving in your speech; for I am
loving and gentle. Speak words that bring life and
knowledge, for I came to bring life and growth,
not death — so do not curse or cause hurt
through your words.

Always take care with your words; curb the evil in the
tongue. Endeavour to speak words that bless,
bring peace, and edify according to the need of
the moment.

Know when to speak and when to keep silent.

Harsh, ungodly words tear down, condemn, wound
deeply, spread like fire, and destroy like cancer.
Gentle and loving words flow like a river of life;
they water hardened ground, soften hardened
hearts, cheering, encouraging, comforting, and
bearing fruit for my kingdom.

1 Timothy 6:6–11 1 John 2:15–17 Mark 4:18,19
Colossians 3:16,17

The world and its desires pass away, but the man who does the will of God lives for ever.
1 John 2:17

L et there be no love of money or of worldly gain in your lives. Be content with enough food, clothing, and shelter. After all, you brought nothing into the world, and you will take nothing out of it.

Allow me to prosper you by guiding you in the ways of godliness and godly living.

A love of the world can be a trap. Worldly desires can lead you away from the gate that leads to eternal life with me, your Saviour. Always be on your guard.

I made the world a beautiful place for you, and because I love you, I want you to play, and to enjoy all parts of my creation. This is all a part of godly living, and brings balance into your lives. But consider your pleasures carefully. They may be very pleasing to you, and seem harmless in themselves. But what is their effect on your walk with me? Do they help you to appreciate my goodness? Or do they hinder discipleship?

Remember: whatever you do, whatever you say, do it for my glory.

**Exodus 14:13,14 1 John 1:7 John 14:12
Psalm 37:4,5**

*The Lord will fight for you; you need only to
be still. Exodus 14:14*

D o not fear, for I am with you, and I will always
help you; just trust in me, my child.

I look at you, and I see you crushed and weighed
down with inner fears and insecurities. This is
why I continually invite you to trust me, to have
faith in your Saviour who drank the cup of death
on the cross, that you may be delivered and set
free in your spirit. I died so that you may walk in
the light, and not be bound by darkness in any
area of your life.

I have delivered believers from lions, from prisons,
from every kind of peril; I have sent food with a
raven. Even in the midst of these perils, they
continued to keep their eyes on me, and trust. If
you would be a vessel for my use, you must have
faith. Believe that I am able and willing to do
greater things, which I have promised to do
through my disciples.

Open your heart to receive me and all that I bring.
Expect me to fulfil your desires and do great
things through you. There is no limit to what I will
do through a believing heart and a childlike trust.

Matthew 17:20   2 Corinthians 12:9,10
Romans 8:36,37

The Lord is good, a refuge in times of trouble.
He cares for those who trust in him.
Nahum 1:7

The deepest form of prayer to your Father is silent trust. The highest form of worship is an unwavering faith in me, the slain Lamb, your risen Christ.

Mary worshipped me as she poured out the perfume on my feet. You worship me with the incense of trust and the perfume of faith.

When you have faith in me, when you believe in my word, you can move mountains, and you make a highway for your God.

I am your stronghold, your strength; and remember, it is my strength that is made perfect in weakness. It is when you are weakest, when your own strength fails you, when you look to me, give all to me, become one with me and trust, that you are made strong.

Move on in obedience and submission, bearing my light, penetrating darkness, spreading my love, joy, and peace, bringing hope, and setting captives free.

**John 10:1–18 Isaiah 40:11 Psalm 23:1–4
Psalm 107:28–31**

*He tends his flock like a shepherd. Isaiah
40:11*

I am your good shepherd. I lay down my life for you.
Never be afraid of me, for I am gentle and caring.
Follow me in simple trust.

I will lead you to green pasture. When the winds blow,
when the storm rages, and the rocky ledge
becomes narrow, follow me simply, without stress
or strain within. Where necessary, I will carry the
lambs in my arms.

Always walk close to me; trust me to guide and protect
you when you can't see the way. You are my
sheep; I faithfully tend my flock, and if even one
should stray, then I will go after that sheep and
bring it back to the fold.

I am your good shepherd; I love my sheep; I serve my
sheep. Follow me in faith. Even though I lay
down my life for you, you don't always trust me,
and this grieves me.

Ponder on my infinite love, and allow your faith to be
put into effect through your obedience to the
voice of your good shepherd.

Psalm 13:5,6   Romans 1:5,6   John 15:16,17

I trust in your unfailing love; my heart rejoices in your salvation. Psalm 13:5

When you love me, it is because you trust me. To trust me is to love me.

My children, the keynote is always trust. Trust is the basic principle — it is the seed planted for harvest.

Think of it as the beginning of a tender shoot that will grow and bloom in all its fullness; it produces a glorious bloom, spreading a fragrance and maturing to bear abundant fruit.

The fragrance of trust is love, tender and strong. To love is to have faith in the one you love, an undying faith that bears the fruit of total submission and obedience. Faith and the love that comes from it are worship to your God; they bear a rich harvest of fruit for my kingdom.

My child, trust me, and love me and your brothers and sisters; go forth and bear fruit for me.

Exodus 15:2 Zephaniah 3:17 Philippians 2:5–8

The Lord your God is with you, he is mighty to save. Zephaniah 3:17

I am your strength and your song; I am your faithful mighty Saviour; I have come to you in the form of a servant; I am Jesus, the Christ.

The ground may appear hard and dry, as you long for rest in your soul, for refreshment. I am your rest, your hiding place, your helper who never leaves you.

During the times you are unfaithful to me, when you lack trust, when you lack the courage to take that step into greater obedience, when your words and actions are not totally in love, then I still remain faithful to you.

I am always present, your faithful watchman, who guards you and keeps you safe from the destroyer and thief. Trust me as I lead you through dry places, across the desert.

Let the knowledge of my love support you. Allow your trust in me to bring peace, and the songs of joy to ring within your heart, bringing refreshment to your soul.

Isaiah 40:12–25   John 1:1–18   Luke 2:4–14
Romans 12:9–21

Grace and truth came through Jesus Christ.
John 1:17

You see my creation around you. It was I who measured the waters, marked off the heavens, held the dust of the earth, and weighed the mountains.

Consider, too, my compassion and gentleness, and my self-sacrificing love. I came into the world to bring light into darkness, to bring grace and truth, to set you free from the power of sin.

I came as a baby, born into poverty and obscurity. My first bed was upon a little pile of hay within a barn. Yet I was the Christchild, your King and Creator. I lived among you, worked long and hard, and walked weary miles. Later, I drank of the cup from the Father who sent me. I was obedient to the point of death. Yes, all this and more I have done for you, my child.

All I ask in return is that you trust in me, and let my love for you show itself in love for others.

Matthew 6:34   Psalm 18:1–3   Hebrews 2:18

The Lord is my rock, my fortress and my deliverer. Psalm 18:1

___

Trust me through each day; allow a growing trust and faith to become a daily adventure, a gradual climb to greater heights of service in my name. Live one day at a time. Say to me: 'Lord, I will trust you through this day'.

I am always with you, and I see the willing heart. I am your fortress, your strength, your faithful guide; I am immovable and dependable.

I never leave you. I am with you when you feel my presence and hear my silent voice. I am with you when you hear nothing, when I seem to be so far away. I am with you, too, when there appears to be only darkness, temptation, and turmoil, and you feel that I have forsaken you.

But my word promises: 'I will never forsake you'. Live by faith in my word; do not rely on your feelings. When you are tempted, as I too was tempted, speak out my word into the darkness.

My child, because of my love and my life given for you, you have the victory.

**Romans 8:1–3   James 1:2–8   Ephesians 4:25,26
Psalm 51:15–17**

*There is now no condemnation for those who
are in Christ Jesus. Romans 8:1*

There is no condemnation for you who belong to
me. Do not despair when you fall during trial; do
not condemn yourself when you make error. My
child, I don't condemn you.

Consider the small child learning to walk — the
struggle, the desire to achieve perfection. It's like
that as you learn to walk with me.

All I ask for is trust in me; I will sanctify you and
complete your love and obedience. Without me
you can do nothing that would glorify my name.

It is not sin when you experience the human emotions
of hurt and anger. But never let the sun go down
on your anger. Walk the way of the cross, as you
spread the good news. It is a way of struggle,
patience, and perseverance. Remember: even I
fell under the weight of my cross.

I am always with you. Trust me, and offer me a
humble, lowly, and contrite heart.

Philippians 4:1   Romans 4:18–25
Philippians 3:7–11

It is God who works in you to will and to act according to his good purpose. Philippians 2:13

Always stand firm in me, your Lord and Saviour. Fight the good fight of faith with courage and perseverance.

My child, keep your eyes on me, my word, and my promises. My power is great, but I am also gentle and caring. I beckon and draw — I never force or push.

Have faith in my power; it is the power of the resurrection — the same power that raised me from the dead.

I see struggle, I see tears; never despair, but allow me to dry those tears.

Trust me in times of sorrow and darkness; although the clouds may appear heavy and low, the sunshine will soon show through; a beam of light will appear, and you will rejoice.

Trust me; I work within you according to my good purposes, and you will indeed see fruit of your patient labour and obedience.

1 Corinthians 16:13,14   Hebrews 4:14–16
1 Corinthians 15:20–26

*Be strong and courageous ... Do not be
afraid or discouraged, for the Lord God, my
God, is with you. 1 Chronicles 28:2*

Be strong and let your heart take courage. Be
strong in my strength; allow my Spirit within you
to guide you in whatever happens.

Sometimes the way will be smooth; sometimes your
faith in me will be tested. In exercising your faith
muscles, you become strong in me. But always
remember that I live within my faithful children.

Allow each day to be a pilgrimage that you and I take
together, in harmony, quietly, surely, with your
footsteps covering mine.

My child, trust the one who is within you; my grace is
always with you. That is why I came into the
world. My death overcame separation and
enabled me to establish my kingdom on earth —
a kingdom where my love lives, where I reign in
your midst.

Yield totally to my love within you, and live on in this
love.

**Matthew 13:18–23   John 4:14   Luke 17:5,6
John 15:1–8**

*I am the vine; you are the branches. If a man
remains in me and I in him, he will bear much
fruit; apart from me you can do nothing. John
15:5*

I n your response to me, do not be like spring's first
bloom — eager to open to my love, bursting out
for a little while in glorious splendour, but then
finally wilting, falling, and dying.

Your life of faith in me must be like an evergreen,
always seeking more depth to grow, spreading
and establishing strong roots, yielding abundant
fruit for me.

I am the gardener. It is I who will prune and nurture the
growing plant, and till the hardened soil. It is I,
your Saviour, who have given so much for you,
who will water with the living water.

Be passive to your gardener's hand; have faith, and
you will grow to stand strong against the winds,
the dry times, and the winter cold. You will bear
much fruit for me.

John 14:16,17 Romans 1:4–6 Matthew 11:28,29

Peace I leave with you; my peace I give you.
John 14:27

D o you feel empty, alone, and lost? When I made
you, I reserved a place within you for your King
and Comforter to dwell. In fact, you cannot live
without me. But I do not force myself on you; you
have the freedom to reject my love and drift
aimlessly in your own strength, instead of
surrendering to me.

How I long to fill my children and bless you with the
many gifts I have to provide. Accept my peace,
and let me increase your faith and love.

Use the power that I provide to take a step in faith, a
step that leads you beyond the door of doubt and
confusion, into a dwelling place of safety and
rest. I am that dwelling place, the ever faithful
One, your safety and rest; I am your Lord and
Saviour.

I ask that we be one — that is, you in me, and I in
you. Surrender your will to mine, and step into
freedom and abundance.

Luke 1:26–38 Matthew 12:50 Romans 15:13

*My soul glorifies the Lord and my spirit
rejoices in God my Saviour. Luke 1:46,47*

The deepest expression of your love for me is
submission to the will of the Father. There are
many times when this requires great courage.
Through your faith in me, you need to draw upon
my strength.

Look at Mary, my mother. Consider her momentary
fear when the angel first spoke to her. In her
humanness, it was unthinkable for her to bear a
child while not yet married.

But Mary had faith. Lifting her heart to God, she spoke
her words of trust and surrender. She was willing
to undergo suffering and humiliation. Through my
grace she was given a courage and strength
beyond her own. Amid suffering she experienced
my peace and joy.

Be ready and willing to share in my suffering, if that is
the will of the Father. Mary received grace and
strength. I am with you, too, as you trust in me.

Hebrews 4:14–16   Psalm 37:27,28   Romans 8:1–3
1 John 1:8,9

Let us then approach the throne of grace with
confidence, so that we may receive mercy
and find grace to help us in our time of need.
Hebrews 4:16

Do not fear your weaknesses, do not run from
  yourself; rather, with me, face your inner self.

I know your struggle; so acknowledge your hidden sin,
  confess it, hand it over to me, and I will free and
  heal you of its bondage.

My fragile one, above all, do not condemn yourself. It
  is up to me to condemn and to forgive, and I
  forgive you. I accept you and love you, and I
  know where you are.

Come to your Redeemer; come to me humbly and
  honestly. I pardon all. I will renew you in mind
  and spirit, if you are willing.

In and through me, gain a new quality of life, a new
  assurance, renewed confidence. Drawing on my
  strength, pursue all that is good, and flee from
  evil.

I'm your fount and spring — everything you have and
  everything you need flows from me. All I give, I
  freely give.

**Psalm 33:1–3   John 1:11–13   Ephesians 6:18
1 Peter 4:13–16**

*The Lord is my light and my salvation —
whom shall I fear? Psalm 27:1*

Let your heart rejoice; be glad that you are a child of God. You are part of my family, my own special child.

Always consider me as your own personal Lord. Have faith in me, and let my love flow through you in love and service to others.

It is you and other believers I choose to work through; you are channels for my love and power. I use your prayers, so pray without ceasing. Let your prayer rise as continual silent trust from the heart. Be passive — simply put your trust in me.

Learn to be patient; be glad, rejoice, and give thanks when you face hindrances, trials, and any obstacle.

Use circumstances to grow steadfast in me, to bear more fruit for my kingdom. Accept all things as permitted by me and coming from my hand. Trust in me without anxiety, and in doing so, gain the blessing of serenity.

Matthew 4:18–20 1 Timothy 1:12–16
Matthew 9:36–38 John 8:31–37

Because of the Lord's great love we are not consumed, for his compassions never fail.
Lamentations 3:22

Follow me — come, follow me! Let my tender mercy be an invitation.

My invitation is extended to all, yet, sadly, few accept it. Many are afraid of total commitment to me — and yet I am always with you, to support you.

I desire all to partake of my love, forgiveness, and mercy, and I want to reach others through you.

There are many fields awaiting harvest — so many souls struggling to be free and in need of my salvation. The lost cry in their wilderness — they search for peace, truth, and love.

Bear my light, take them truth, and end their search for the right way. In my name release them from struggle, panic, and pain.

There is praise and rejoicing when even one lost soul is found, and receives my truth and salvation.

Deuteronomy 33:26,27   James 1:17
Mark 12:10,11   1 John 4:18

The eyes of the Lord range throughout the earth to strengthen those whose hearts are fully committed to him. 2 Chronicles 16:9

D o not be afraid when I guide you toward new and unfamiliar pathways. Remember: you are not alone — I walk by your side, so rest in my love and power, which is without variation or shifting shadow.

I am the unchangeable one — the rock, and the stone which was rejected. Don't reject me, too, by failing to trust me by letting fear come between us.

Desire a heart that yields to my perfect love and strength. Let there be trust and submission; abandon yourself to my will. Abandon yourself so that my will on earth may be manifested and achieved through you.

Open yourself to me more fully. Look to me, and in simple faith receive blessings, blessings which are the fruits of trust and obedience.

1 Thessalonians 3:1–8   1 Peter 4:1,2,13–17
2 Timothy 1:8–12

*Rejoice that you participate in the sufferings
of Christ, so that you may be overjoyed when
his glory is revealed. 1 Peter 4:13*

You experience the pains and uncertainties of life.
   Your existence in the flesh appears to involve a
   complex interchange, and you strive to keep a
   balance.

Those who have surrendered their heart to me, those
   who live by truth, and stand on truth, need never
   be ashamed.

It is indeed better to suffer for doing good than to be
   acclaimed for folly.

To lose for me is to gain. When persecuted for me,
   endure. Count it as joy, and rejoice. When you
   are insulted and scorned for me, you will receive
   the crown of righteousness.

Stand tall; stand firm; stand in my name; stand on my
   truth; stand in my strength; stand in
   righteousness. Stand in faith. Stand for me.

**Matthew 26:38–42   Psalm 121   Isaiah 53:11,12
Psalm 27:8,9**

*I desire to do your will, O my God; your law is
within my heart. Psalm 40:8*

D elight to do the will of the Father.

As I knelt before the Father in the Garden of
Gethsemane, my mind was focusing on all that
lay before me. My human nature recoiled at the
pain and suffering to which I had to submit
myself.

As I called on my Father in prayer, as I lifted up my
eyes to heaven, I was able to perceive the victory
that only submission and obedience could bring.

My spirit soared, my Father's angel strengthened me,
and I was able to face the mighty victory ahead.

All this was done for you; I bore the suffering instead
of you. When you trust in me, you share my
victory.

So, my child, seek God's face, and delight to do the
will of the Father who sent me.

Psalm 19:1–4   Psalm 104:5–13   Genesis 1:1–5

You are worthy, our Lord and God, to receive glory and honour and power, for you created all things, and by your will they were created and have their being. Revelation 4:11

Look around you, my child; the whole earth speaks of my glory.

From the smallest, most fragile flower, to the greatest flowing river; from the smallest fish in the rivers and seas, to the great mountains, where a deer shelters her fawn from the snow; I have made them all, and they all tell of my glory.

Thunder, lightning, rushing wind, delicate beauty, and awesome greatness I give to you.

The power of my spirit supports all, creates all. All life stems from me — all is a part of me.

See me in the whole world, in the earth and all its fruits.

Allow me, your Creator and your Redeemer, to minister to you through all my creation.

Acts 6:7–15   1 Corinthians 2:1–5
1 Corinthians 15:10   Galatians 5:16–26

Do you not know that your body is a temple of the Holy Spirit, who is in you, whom you have received from God? You are not your own; you were bought at a price.
1 Corinthians 6:19,20

D o not be afraid to live and speak my truth before other people, but remember that I am always with you.

In obedience and trust, filled with my spirit, take the gospel message to the hungry, the lost, and the bound.

Proclaim the good news; do not fear rebuff. Tell people that they are free through Christ crucified, and that I've already paid the ransom.

Know, too, my child, that it is not the spirit of the world or the things of the world that bless, but only the Spirit and power of God.

All grace, all fruit, all gifts are given to you from God the Father, through Christ Jesus.

Ephesians 4:1–3   James 5:8–10
1 Corinthians 3:16   1 John 4:19,20

Whoever wants to be first must be your slave
— just as the Son of Man did not come to be
served, but to serve, and to give his life as a
ransom for many. Matthew 20:27,28

B ring a ray of my light each day to someone.

Greet your brothers and sisters with an attitude of love, joy, and peace. I urge you, always be patient; realise that when you greet others, you greet me, and when you serve others, you serve me.

I may stand before you in the form of a lowly, broken image. Do not turn from me; do not judge; do not be like a Pharisee.

If you love me, then be ready to serve those whom I send you to serve. Be ready to love and help your humblest brothers and sisters.

You are my holy temple. I live within you, so serve my people with Christlikeness.

Treasure the words of the Lord in your heart — they are more precious than the finest gold and sweeter than honey.